TAILS YOU WIN

TAILS YOU WIN

TAILS YOU WIN

AN ANTHROPOMORPHIC A TO Z OF DOGS

In original verse by
Gill Rowe

Line drawings by Jennifer Taggart

The Book Guild Ltd

First published in Great Britain in 2020 by
The Book Guild Ltd
9 Priory Business Park
Wistow Road, Kibworth
Leicestershire, LE8 0RX
Freephone: 0800 999 2982
www.bookguild.co.uk
Email: info@bookguild.co.uk
Twitter: @bookguild

Copyright © 2019 Gill Rowe

The right of Gill Rowe to be identified as the author of this
work has been asserted by her in accordance with the
Copyright, Design and Patents Act 1988.

All rights reserved. No part of this publication may be
reproduced, transmitted, or stored in a retrieval system, in any form or by any means,
without permission in writing from the publisher, nor be otherwise circulated in
any form of binding or cover other than that in which it is published and without
a similar condition being imposed on the subsequent purchaser.

Typeset in Garamond Premier Pro

Printed and bound in the UK by TJ International, Padstow, Cornwall

ISBN 978 1913208 059

British Library Cataloguing in Publication Data.
A catalogue record for this book is available from the British Library.

For Brambles

Acknowledgements

With grateful thanks to Tom Stacey for reading the manuscript, Robin Nott for his advice, Jenny Taggart for her lovely line drawings and, above all, to Clive for his unfailing encouragement and support.

Contents

Foreword	x
Afghan Hound	1
Airedale Terrier	3
Bagel Hound	4
Basset Hound	5
Beagle	7
Bulldog	9
Cairn Terrier	10
Cavalier King Charles Spaniel	11
Cockapoo	13
Cocker Spaniel	16
Cross Breed Confection	18
Dachshund	19
Dalmatian	21
Elkhound	24

English Setter	26
French Poodle	28
Golden Retriever	30
Greyhound	32
Havanese	33
Irish Wolfhound	34
Jack Russell Terrier	36
King Charles Spaniel	38
Labradoodle	40
Labrador	42
Lhasa Apso	44
Maltese	46
Miniature Dachshund	47
Mongrel (Heinz)	50
Norwich Terrier	52
Old English Sheepdog (Dulux)	53
Pekinese	55
Pekinese Folderol	57
Pointer	59
Poodle	60

Pug	62
Puggle	64
Reflections from a Hybrid	66
Rhodesian Ridgeback	67
Scottish Terrier	68
Shih Tzu	70
Springer Spaniel	71
Tibetan Terrier	73
Tosa	75
Uruguayan Cimarron	76
Vizsla	78
West Highland White Terrier	79
Whippet	81
Xoloitzcuintil	83
Yorkshire Terrier	85
Zuchon	87
Postscript: Turn Me Around	88

Foreword

When nothing much else is happening
I curl up and take a rest.
I don't fritter precious energy.
We dogs know best.

I greet each day as a chance to play
So I never get depressed.
I don't indulge in introspection.
We dogs know best.

Each offer of healthy exercise
I embrace with zeal and zest.
I relish the fresh air in my lungs.
We dogs know best.

I value genuine affection.
I enjoy it when caressed
And I show my appreciation.
We dogs know best.

By glamour and extravagance
I am hugely unimpressed.
I'm content with simple pleasures.
We dogs know best.

I greet friends enthusiastically
For one's love should be expressed.
I would never feign indifference.
We dogs know best.

My empathetic sense is keen;
I feel when you're distressed.
And I let you know I'm with you.
We dogs know best.

~

Devoted, loyal, affectionate,
Love beating in his chest,
Attend to what he's telling you:
The heart knows best.

Afghan Hound

You will know me, by sight;
See my proud, regal air.
I have an abundance
Of long, silky hair.
I'm lovely to look at;
I'm turned out in style.
My stylist will say my
Toilette takes a while!

I look like a film star,
But aeons ago
I used to hunt leopards in
The wild and the snow.
I turn on a sixpence,
I fly through the air.
I am a demon for speed.
For sloth I don't care.

The tip of my tail forms
An in reverse 'C'.
Although not belonging,
Uniquely, to me,
I'm pleased with this feature.
Afghan is my breed.
I win accolades for
Both beauty and speed.

Airedale Terrier

I am known as the King of Terriers
Because I'm impressively large.
No other terrier can touch me;
I am always the one to take charge.

My black and tan coat's short and wiry,
I always stand proud, tail erect.
My legs, long and straight, are powerful.
My confident air commands respect.

Unlike some of those smaller terriers,
Who all have an 'end up' to keep,
I don't pick fights, you'll not hear me yap.
My bark's pleasant, melodious and deep.

My origins lie in West Yorkshire
In the vale of the fair River Aire.
I'm a proud Airedale. I am the boss.
To challenge me, no one would dare!

Bagel Hound

First things first: I am not edible.
I bear no resemblance to a bun.
My parents disapproved of my name
Which doesn't do justice to either one.
My dad is a handsome Basset Hound,
My mum is a Beagle, nimble and swift.
I have the best from both of my parents.
For me, being a Bagel's a gift.

I have a very expressive face,
With soulful, arresting brown eyes.
My long ears are soft and stroke-able.
A short time ago, to my huge surprise,
I acquired celebrity status;
You will see me on children's TV,
Where my standing is stellar; I'm the
Blue Peter dog. It's true. Tune in and see!

Basset Hound

I've folds of skin on my short legs,
My ears are smooth, and very long.
My sense of smell is awesome,
I'm quite extraordinarily strong.

Speed's never been my strong point,
Though I'm used for hunting hares.
(My only chance of catching one
Is to take it unawares).

So, unlike most other hunters,
My progress is quite slow.
But my nose will always show
The pack just where it's best to go.

Out hunting, people help me
To clamber over stone walls.
Huntsmen and field are all on foot.
The thrill of it never palls.

Half-way between two breeds of hound,
(The Bloodhound and the Beagle)
There is me; I am a Basset Hound.
I am fearless as an eagle.

Beagle

My eye is keen, my tail is up,
My sense of smell
Acute.

My pedigree is awesome; of
Pure breeding I'm
The fruit.

I chase the hare across the fields,
Men leaping in
Pursuit.

I love to hunt when with the pack,
But I am not
A brute.

For I appeal to royalty,
And palace life
I suit.

I may become the new 'must have'
Since Meghan finds
Me cute!

Bulldog

My name is not Winston.
I don't smoke a cigar.
But you'll know who I am
Wherever you are.

My chest's very broad.
I've a large lower jaw
With pendulous jowls
(What they're for I'm not sure).

I know that I'm someone
Commanding respect.
The proud British Bulldog
You never can neglect.

Cairn Terrier

My ears are pricked.
My nose a-twitch.
I'm on the case.
Cave!

I have no fears.
I'll split your ears.
You hear that bark?
That's me.

But as for you.
You can't get through
Because of me.
Yippee!

Cairn Terrier, I.
You'll not get by.
You want a fight?
Try me!

Cavalier King Charles Spaniel

Ravissante, insouciante and *elegante* am I.
A Spaniel, Cavalier King Charles. Black, white and tan – a Tri..

Enjoying royal favour at King Charles's Restoration,
We have, as you'd imagine, achieved a certain station.
Our ancestors were present at the *levées* of Old Rowley
(That's why we are accustomed to being roused but slowly).

Royal approval naturally won us privilege and status
And ever since it's simply been impossible to hate us.

Habitually, we wear a smile and wave a feathered tail.
It always works because, you see, good manners will prevail.

My distinguished Blenheim cousins are most numerous in the clan,
But some of us are redheads, and others black and tan.
We're all delightful and engaging. Our appeal will never die.
But the *primus inter pares* is the Tricolour, or Tri..

I am *elegante*, *insouciante* and *ravissante*, and why?
I'm a Cavalier to my tail-tip. I could not tell a lie!

Cockapoo

I'm a cockapoo called Baxter.
I am only four months old.
My master thinks he's teaching me
To do as I am told.

Sometimes I will oblige him
To make him think he's right.
But I get up to lots of tricks
When he is out of sight.

It is boring when I'm left alone,
Though all my toys are new.
When there isn't any company,
I find something good to chew.

I am very fond of chair legs,
The best are made of oak.
They are satisfying things to gnaw
And never make me choke.

I'm also fond of playing ball,
A tennis ball's the best,
I like to chase and pounce on it,
Then kill it off, the pest.

I don't like all the grooming
That I'm subjected to.
I'm washed and brushed and combed too much
But if good, I get a chew.

I need these little extras
For my food is a bit sad.
Just boring doggo pellets,
Though the flavour isn't bad.

I am lucky with my master
Whose affection is plain to see.
But he does insist I piddle outside,
Which is a mystery to me.

He gets in a most frightful tizz
If I do perform inside.
I don't understand his problem.
To be truthful, I haven't tried.

But mostly we get on just fine,
Young Master Tom and me.
As for what will happen next,
Well, just you wait and see!

Cocker Spaniel

I come in two versions. One is more showy,
But both have luxuriant, long, silky hair.
My legs and my tail have smart, waving feathers.
My grooming takes patience and long hours of care.

I could give Joseph a run for his money;
My amazing coat comes in a wide choice of hue:
Black, liver, tan and white, red, golden, blue roan,
Chocolate, to mention but only a few.

You may, by now, have guessed that I'm a Spaniel;
A Cocker. When working I'm trained for the gun.
When being shown, my performance is stylish.
I've lost count of how many prizes I've won.

Perhaps, above all, I'm a lovable pet;
Affectionate, loyal, always ready to play.
I'm known for possessing a great sense of fun.
What more could you possibly ask for? Please say!

Cross Breed Confection

My legs are flecked like a Spaniel's,
My thick hair is silkily soft,
But my heart is as brave as Daniel's
And I'm razor-sharp aloft.

My pedigree should be treasured;
The DNA's uniquely fab..
For my Collie mum was pleasured
By the visiting thatcher's Lab..

I'm a long-haired Labradollie,
A brand that may yet succeed.
Thanks, Ma. Your moment of folly
Makes me first of a new rare breed!

Dachshund

My back is long,
My legs are short,
My tummy is near
To the ground.

I am plucky.
I like hunting,
But not in a pack.
Not this hound.

In days of old,
I was sent down
Holes, after badgers
Underground.

With spade-like paws
I'd dig like mad
Into the new sett that
I had found.

Then down I'd go,
Flush out the foe,
To badger him up
Above ground.

These days, you'll find
If I'm your pet,
I am cheerful, loyal,
Oh, so sound!

But (it's my genes)
If shown a hole
I'll dig, sniffing out
Below ground!

Dalmatian

My appearance is distinctive;
No other looks like me.
My lovely white coat is spotted;
The finest you could see.

Our beautiful breed became famous
Because of a children's story,
Which featured one hundred and one
Of us. I bask in reflected glory!

Yes, I'm a noble Dalmatian,
The very finest breed.
Should you seek an aristocrat,
I am the one you need.

Don't you just love the fine spattering of spots!
All over the white coat they're sprinkled like petals.
Try to count them, you'll find your brain tied up in knots.

Each dog has its very own pattern of dots,
So identification's never a problem.
Don't you just love the fine spattering of spots!

Sometimes a few merge together in blots,
So the general impression is darker.
Try to count them, you'll find your brain tied up in knots.

Please observe the elegant way that he trots.
He perfected this back in his carriage dog days.
Don't you just love the fine spattering of spots!

He's a Dalmatian. He's good-looking and bright.
His black spots (sometimes liver) a marvellous sight.
Don't you just love his fine spattering of spots,
Try to count them, you'll find your brain tied up in knots!

Elkhound

I am Norwegian, athletic and strong.
My stamina's great, my history long.
For the Vikings, so many ages ago,
I hunted elk in the tundra and snow.

In Nordic legends, it is recorded,
I stood down a wolf pack (much applauded).
I've also been known to hunt lions and bears,
My services better than traps and snares.

Loud barking is deep in my DNA.
While stopping the animals running away,
By leaping and feinting, I always barked hard,
Showing the huntsmen where I was on guard.

I still hunt for elk (known elsewhere as moose).
I am bold. I'd say more than just 'boo' to a goose!
You'll more likely find me as somebody's pet.
But the joy of a good bark I'll never forget!

I've a very thick coat, a tightly curled tail,
Pricked ears and a nose for elk which cannot fail.
I've mentioned already my bark, which is loud.
Norway's National Dog, I am naturally proud.

English Setter

I'm a very special type of working gun dog.
I have some attributes not given to the rest.
My generic name is Setter,
But I'm English, none is better;
No, my particular version is the best!

I am sometimes known as Lavarack or Llewellyn,
Which were names of famous 19th century strains.
We were trained to hunt by scent,
Then stop dead and 'point', which meant
We'd found the hiding birds; the huntsmens' gains.

You will find my coat is mostly white in colour,
But smartly flecked, with fringed and feathered legs and tail.
My Irish cousins, to a man,
Sport red. The Gordons black and tan.
With any one of us, your game-hunting cannot fail.

French Poodle

There's a delightful English couple
In the room next door to me.
We communicate infrequently
But we're *en rapport*, we three.

We first fell into conversation
Only the other day.
She'd let drop a piece of *croissant*,
Which I couldn't let get away!

You may wonder why I noticed it,
Or how I came to see
When they've put a great big canvas screen
Between each balcony.

The truth is I was peckish.
I'd been up for hours and hours,
And though they were having breakfast
There was no sign of ours.

So I drew to their attention
The dropped *patisserie*,
And being English and *bien élevés*
They gave it all to me.

≈

Were you to wander *à la plage*
Around about *midi*,
You'd see a coiffed and manicured
White French poodle. That is me!

Golden Retriever

I'm amiable and serene,
You'll never see me frown.
For I am always happy,
In country or in town.

By training, I'm a gun dog,
The country suits me best.
But I'm content anywhere
I go, at my pet's behest.

The men who go shooting birds
Rely on my expertise.
I rush to retrieve their game;
I always love to please.

I am quite unflappable.
My 'cool' can soothe the nerves
Of stressed out city workers.
I love all whom it serves.

My silky coat is golden,
My expressive eyes dark brown.
Whatever life may throw at me,
It will never get me down.

Greyhound

If it's speed you're after, I'm the one for you!
There's not another breed to touch me. That is true.
With legs straining, ears flat, slender arching back,
I compete with other greyhounds round a track.
I am comparable, they tell me, to a race horse,
Which is trained to race its rivals round a course.
Men bet on our speed, which always cuts a dash.
In both cases, foolish humans waste a lot of cash!

Havanese

I am quite outrageously pretty;
I could bring a strong man to his knees!
I am stroke-able, fluffily soft to the touch.
What am I? A cute Havanese.

Some say I resemble my cousin,
Also fluffy and small – the Maltese.
But my beautiful coat is far silkier,
Which explains our relative fees!

My homeland is far off, in Cuba,
But wherever I go I will please.
Children all love me. Some think I'm a toy.
They pet me, but don't dare to tease.

For mine is a noble, superior breed
(Though this truth not everyone sees).
So, now that you know, next year at Crufts
Look out for a cute Havanese.

Irish Wolfhound

I am an Irish Wolfhound,
Mascot to the Irish Guards.
My important title ensures
That I hold all of the cards.

I am friendly, large and charming.
I don't hunt wolves any more.
My dignified demeanour ensures
That for me people open the door.

When there is some special day
With Guardsmen all on parade,
Guess who meets the Colonel
In Chief? Yes, me. I have it made!

Last week I met his Duchess,
Who charmed me with her smile.
I really felt that the two of us
Were champions of elegant style.

On this last St. Patrick's day,
I wore a shamrock, she wore green.
Between the two of us, for sure,
Didn't we both light up the scene!

Jack Russell Terrier

Smooth-haired or rough,
Both sorts are tough.
We're speedy; see
Us run!

I hunt for rats,
I take on cats.
Fighting, for me,
Is fun.

Some get their kicks
From circus tricks,
Or shin up trees
For fun.

With gifts like these
We aim to please,
Though different,
Each one.

You seek a breed?
If 'spunk' you need,
Jack Russell is
The one.

King Charles Spaniel

Yesterday, I went to church,
Where the vicar smiled at me.
I went right to the altar rail.
I'm a King Charles Spaniel, see.

I can go just where I please.
They will waive the entrance fee
To country houses and the like
Because they can see it's me.

I have a royal licence
From the highest in the land;
That is my pet, good King Charles,
The Second, you understand.

I am a true free spirit.
You'll find me hard to train.
Old Rowley quite indulged me
Throughout his glorious reign.

You'll see me in some portraits.
I'm not quite the same today.
My nose is far less pointed,
But you'll know me, right away.

Though I'm a royal person,
Don't make a hullabaloo.
I'm not proud or stuffy. See,
I'm waving my tail at you!

Labradoodle

I am, now, very fashionable.
I'll be at all the smartest places,
Whether out to lunch in London
Or possibly at the races.

I've come to dislike the camera;
I've been photographed so often.
Just seeing the image is enough
To make hardened features soften.

For it seems that people love me.
Perhaps they like my tousled look.
I'm very like a woolly lamb. My owner
Should have a shepherd's crook!

My parentage is interesting.
Gun dog meets movie star!
I have the best genes from both;
You'll love me, wherever you are.

Father's post-script

Because I'm obliging and meek,
Unlike that small creature, the Peke,
I've been teamed up with others
With whom, though dog brothers,
A relationship I'd never seek.

Of all the breeds under the sun,
The Poodle emerged as the one
To be offered my genes.
The result of which means
That all Labradoodles are fun.

As for the dear Labradollie,
As sweet as a fruit juice ice lolly,
Well, that was, I confess
(Though more, rather than less)
Not wholly the fault of the Collie!

Labrador

I'm obliging and obedient.
I've been trained not to be deviant.
On a shoot you'll find I'm perfectly
Behaved.

But I have a little weakness;
For all my apparent meekness,
When it comes to food, my appetite's
Depraved.

Scavenging's my favourite sport.
I pinch more than a good dog ought.
Dustbins and compost heaps are my
Delight!

Since for food I'm always yearning,
I'm completely undiscerning.
If it's edible, there's nothing I
Won't grab.

I may suffer from halitosis.
But never from neurosis.
Unflappable, dependable, I'm
A Lab..

Lhasa Apso

I was bred for a peaceful, temple life.
In that quiet, Buddhist world there is no strife.
There, I learned the art of meditation.
Many an hour was spent in contemplation.

Now, as then, you'll find my nature is serene.
I have the regal bearing of a queen.
My double coat, which tumbles to the ground,
Is silky. I am quite unlike a hound.

My ears, which are long, fall over my face,
Making it hard to take part in a race.
My nose is quite short; I may sometimes snore.
If reluctant, I pin myself flat to the floor.

Unusually, mine is an indoor breed.
No sport is for me. I haven't the speed.
I'm a good guard, by nature protective.
My hearing is keen. I bark invective.

Aeons ago, I was born in Tibet.
I'm a Lhasa Apso. These days I'm a pet.
There is one thing I should, perhaps, mention –
I expect deference, and lots of attention!

Maltese

I look glamorous and high maintenance.
I take luxurious living in my stride.
I like the fanciest apartment blocks
In Knightsbridge, Hollywood, Upper East Side.

But I'm also highly intelligent.
I'm friendly, loving and adaptable.
So, though my appearance may be perfect,
With 'normal' life I am compatible.

I am happy to romp with the children;
I love to run a competitive race.
Next time, on your screen, you see me at Crufts,
Please remember I'm not just a cute face!

Miniature Dachshund

My name is Max.
A Wire-haired Dachs.,
The *recherché* miniature version, as you see.
But though I'm small,
And cute and all,
You'd be foolish if you tried to mess with me.

My pets are cool.
Fine, as a rule.
Which is more than can be said about my food.
Yes, here's my lunch.
The biscuits crunch.
But that is all that I can say that isn't rude.

They've been to class.
Some silly ass
Told them not to give me luscious meat and all.
So there it is.
It's all there is.
This boring formula soon begins to pall.

I dig outside.
The garden's wide
And you never know what treasures you may find.
I get up roots.
I eat young shoots.
Well, I need something to get menus off my mind!

I have a plan
To make them ban
That insulting, tasteless, veterinary dross.
I'll eat their plants.
My giddy aunts!
Then they'll soon know that I'm the boss.

Mongrel (Heinz)

My conception was by accident.
My colouring's an experiment.
But I have a lovely temperament.
I'm not rough.

In my genes there's no inbreeding
So I need no special feeding.
I'm robust, a vet I'll not be needing.
I am tough.

Though I'm comical in appearance
With a very low ground clearance,
I'm pretty good at running errands.
I'm a schmooze.

Sometimes people think I am a thug
(I've the worst features of a Pug)
And some would say an ugly mug.
Well, you choose.

My pedigree may be derided,
My slobbery smile is quite lopsided,
But I am hardly ever chided,
As you see.

Who needs to claim gentility
When they have that rare facility
To radiate amiability?
Heinz. That's me.

Norwich Terrier

Like the spire on our ancient cathedral,
My pert ears point up to the sky.
My pedigree's long and distinguished.
A smart Norwich Terrier, I.

Don't confuse me with my Norfolk cousin.
Though at first glance we may look alike
(Brindled coat and short cut-off trousers),
His ear droops. Mine forms a sharp spike.

My job used to be hunting small vermin.
Mostly, these days, I am kept as a pet.
Which isn't to say, if given the chance,
I won't kill any mouse I can get!

Old English Sheepdog (Dulux)

I have the loveliest long, shaggy coat
Which dances and sways in the air when I run.
I leap and I bound with a smile on my face,
You can tell that I'm having good fun!

I know that I must be quite cheering a sight
Whether bouncing around or just sitting still,
With my pink tongue hanging right out of my mouth.
For no-one, anywhere, wishes me ill.

I've been having the time of my life
Since retiring (I used to herd sheep on a farm).
I help advertise paint products on the TV.
I am pampered and groomed and shielded from harm.

Small people love me, although I'm quite large,
For I am endearing and soft to the touch.
You'll have seen me in ads.. I must have made millions
For the makers of 'my' brand of paint. Guess how much!

Pekinese

I've got my special toiletries
In a handsome tartan grip.
There's shampoo and conditioner,
Prescription ointment for my lip.

In the secret inner pocket
You'll find an extra little treat.
For you never can be sure, abroad,
Just what is safe to eat.

This year, I've got a snazzy
New designer bit of kit.
It's a scarf, with matching visor cap.
A really perfect fit.

The only problem I envisage
On hol., *à la Côte d'Azur*,
Is the really quite excessive heat,
Which for me has no allure.

Oh, by the way, I never said;
Just so you know the score,
I'm quite the most enchanting
Pekinese you ever saw!

Pekinese Folderol

You'll see I am a Pekinese, a Pekinese or Peke.
I'm the colour of fine teakinese, teakinese or teak.
When first you hear me speakinese, speakinese or speak,
You'll think that I'm some freakinese, freakinese or freak.

For you'd think I'd speak in Pekinese, Pekinese or Peke,
But in fact I favour Greekinese, Greekinese or Greek.
I learned it from the beakinese, the beakinese or beak
Of a migrant in the creekinese, the creekinese or creek.

A gentle teacher, meekinese, meekinese or meek,
Whom I recommend you seekinese, seekinese or seek.
You may think that I'm some geekinese, geekinese or geek.
No. I'm just a gifted Pekinese, Pekinese or Peke.

Pointer

Not having, like you, a strong index finger
(None of my digital pads has a joint),
I indicate things by different methods;
Using, for instance, my long nose to point.

This isn't, of course, its primary function;
It processes every aroma, scent, smell.
My fine nose alerts me to every nuance,
Not always pleasant, as I know too well!

I'm an experienced, blue-blooded gun dog.
I accompany sportsmen hunting for game.
I can direct them to possible targets.
Who am I? Why, Pointer's the name!

Poodle

My tail is topped with a pom-pom,
Which gives me a frivolous look.
I'm decorative, but not scatty.
You might find my nose in a book.

For I am highly intelligent;
See the keen look in my eye.
My brain is sharp as a razor.
You'll not catch me out. Just you try!

Originally, I was a gun dog.
I've long been a good friend to men.
I've been taken into battle. Once,
I won praise from Napoleon.

Today, I come in three sizes:
Standard, miniature and toy.
I imagine that my ancestors
Would have disliked this ploy.

Whatever our size, you will know us
By our pom-poms and tight curly coats.
When choosing a classy companion,
We Poodles should get the most votes.

Pug

My build's short and squat,
My jaw undershot.
I do wheeze a lot.
I'm a Pug.

I'm strong at my core.
I've wrinkles galore
And, yes, I do snore.
I'm a Pug.

My face is quite flat.
I can run to fat.
I like a nice pat.
I'm a Pug.

I have a sad face,
But I love to race
All over the place.
I'm a Pug.

All kids I adore.
I'll roll on the floor
And make them guffaw.
I'm a Pug.

I've a waddling gait,
Though my legs stand straight.
Rude comments I hate.
I'm a Pug.

My breed is not new
(My blood may be blue).
To you I'll stay true.
I'm a Pug.

Puggle

I am a designer dog, you know.
I rejoice in the name of Puggle,
An elision of my parents' names,
Which involved a bit of a juggle.

My father, a fine hunting Beagle,
Met and fell for a Pug, my mother.
Their progeny, me, has a nice turn of speed;
I always out-run my Pug brother.

Some of the Pug physiognomy
You'll see reflected in my features.
Not, however, my nose, which is Beagle.
I am one of God's luckier creatures.

You won't hear from me that Pug snuffle
(I know, always, when Mother is near!).
My breathing is never restricted.
My airways are beautifully clear.

Sometimes I'm teased for being a hybrid.
But I pay no attention. I know
That my special parentage is stellar,
As a long string of prizes will show.

Reflections from a Hybrid

I'm a Cavghan or an Afgalier.
Depending on where you stand
You'll see Spaniel (front) or Afghan (rear).
For I'm both, you understand.

This illustrates what once I read
In a quantum physics article;
According to how you look, it said,
You'll see either wave or particle.

So here's a truth for all to find;
Things may seem clear to you,
But take care always to bear in mind
There's another point of view.

Rhodesian Ridgeback

I'm a Rhodesian Ridgeback,
Simbo Injha is my name.
My appetite's voracious;
You should see me gobble up game.

Back in Africa, I was trained
To check lions on the roam.
I was my owner's guard dog
Protecting the family home.

I am large, and look imposing.
Some people do take fright
If they meet me when 'on duty',
Particularly at night.

I can be fierce; I'm fearless.
But with children I like to play.
At heart, I'm a gentle giant.
Don't listen to what people say.

Scottish Terrier

You don't see me often;
I'm quite out of vogue,
Because of some rumour
That I am a rogue.

For those 'in the know'
All this is a farce.
I'm quite a looker;
I've been best in class.

Sure, I've a temper.
I'm known to explode
If I see an imposter
On my patch of road.

I've black hair, square jaw
And long, noble nose.
This Scot is proud
Wherever he goes.

Were once we to meet,
What should you expect?
Here is my warning:
Treat me with respect.

Shih Tzu

The stones are hot beneath my feet.
My bow is tied too tight.
The scene upon the hotel beach,
Is not a pretty sight.

A place has been reserved for me,
I'm invited to lie down.
I have towel, water, sun-shade.
Still I wear a little frown.

Many women sport bikinis.
Having shed their outer layers,
They show off their various figures
As if advertising wares.

This dreadful lack of breeding's
Not an option if you're me –
A most superior, white Shih Tzu
Of impeccable pedigree!

Springer Spaniel

I'm bright of eye and keen of mind.
I'm full of bounce and joy.
I'll turn whatever I may find
Into a brand new toy.

Bounding in pursuit, I go,
Of sticks, or balls, or rings.
Across the park, my heart aglow,
I fly as if on wings.

My feathered ears are streaming back,
My pink tongue's hanging out.
Oblivious to indignant quack
Or owner's desperate shout.

It's in my genes, this love of speed,
The need I have to fly.
The mightiest of the Spaniel breed,
I am a Springer, I!

Tibetan Terrier

I have the shaggiest, hearth-rug coat,
A fringe that flops over my eyes
And the sweetest, most sensitive nature,
Which may come as a great surprise.

It's my name which is so misleading;
I'm not really a terrier at all.
My Tibetan name, which is Tsang Apso,
Means shaggy dog, a much better call!

Europeans called me a terrier
Because of my build and my size.
But I predate terriers, you should know,
(Though our wolf genes are well in disguise).

I come in a wide range of colours:
Black, white, brindle, golden or grey.
Which of all these is most beautiful
Is for you, the beholder, to say.

I'm engaging, sensitive, gentle.
Though originally used to the wild,
Once I am part of your family,
You will find I'm your favourite child!

Tosa

You won't see me around,
I'm a mean fighting hound.
I'd be put in a pound
Over here.

I was bred in Japan,
Where there won't be a ban,
For I'm part of a plan.
Over there,

Dog fighting is legal.
I look proud and regal;
But I'm cruel as an eagle.
I've no fear.

If I am called to fight,
I will give all my might.
I'm a formidable sight.
Don't come near.

Uruguayan Cimarron

My name begins, uniquely, with a 'U'.
My breed may well be quite unknown to you.
My history is strange, to say the least;
For many years, I lived as a wild beast.

To Uruguay I came first with the Spanish.
A guard dog, I. But then, one day, they vanish.
I was cast aside, like a threadbare shoe.
Turned out into the wild, what should I do?

We dogs, all abandoned, were left to our fate.
We formed a small pack. I soon found a mate.
We hunted like wolves, a powerful force.
It isn't surprising that I'm full of resource.

I have a broad chest. I am stocky in build.
I don't mind how many creatures I've killed.
These days, once more, we are servants of men.
Captured and tamed, we are guard dogs again.

I'm one of the fiercest dogs on this earth.
Most people, wisely, give me a wide berth.
My curious history shows you I'm feral.
You would stand in my way at your peril!

Vizsla

I'm the smallest of my Pointer cousins.
My nose is pink, my coat a rusty gold.
My fine antecedents are Hungarian.
I've been a hunting dog since days of old.

I'm loyal, gentle and affectionate,
So I am part of the family too.
It's unusual to be gun dog and pet.
I'm glad that hunting isn't all I do!

My nature's serene. I've a calm, quiet air.
By the pressure of showing I am unfazed.
I'm a Vizsla. I have won trophies at Crufts.
Once you have met me, you'll not be amazed.

West Highland White Terrier

I'm a West Highland White,
So, try as you might,
You'll not make me take fright.
I'm a terrier.

I'm bouncy and bright.
My smile's a delight.
On my paws I am light.
I'm a terrier.

I don't always do right;
I may pick a fight.
But I guard through the night.
I'm a terrier.

Though I am short in height,
For me it's no plight.
My breeding's quite right.
I'm a terrier.

If involved in a fight,
I'll not be contrite
If I happen to bite.
I'm a terrier.

I'm a West Highland White,
A beautiful sight.
But do get this right;
I'm a terrier.

Whippet

I carry no fat.
My stomach is flat.
There's not much to pat
On me.

I'm thin as a pin.
I don't raid the bin.
That isn't the sin
For me.

I might just break out
If chocolate's about.
That makes my pet shout
At me.

Others may moan
I look skin and bone,
But there's perfect tone
On me.

This fast racing hound
Will cover the ground
In bound after bound.
See me!

The Whippet's my breed.
I revel in speed.
It fills a real need
In me.

Xoloitzcuintil

I come in three sizes,
With hair, or without.
Back with the Aztecs
I wielded some clout.
Much given to thought,
I wrinkle my brow
When using my brain.
I am doing so now.

But it's my nature
That earns me my fame.
Known often as Xolo
(Which is not my real name),
You'll find me trusty,
Both loving and loyal.
One day, p'raps, I'll be
Owned by a Royal.

Meanwhile I am happy,
Just contented to be
A Xoloitzcuintil.
Call me Xolo; that's me.

Yorkshire Terrier

You might see me in a quilted coat,
My hair washed and brushed with care.
Sometimes, my poor besotted owner
Will even tie a ribbon in my hair.

I often travel in a handbag
From which I survey the scene.
I may look like a childish toy,
But my intelligence is keen.

My name is somewhat misleading;
(Think moors, cricket, tough Northern grit).
My rugged forebears would turn in their graves
If they saw my contemporary kit.

For I am a Yorkshire Terrier.
I've abandoned my county of old
To become a soft, pampered Southerner.
I, for one, simply can't stand the cold!

Zuchon

You have no idea how special I am!
My cross breeding has made me unique.
When a Bichon Frise and a Shih Tsu combined,
There was I, an adorable freak.

I've the dark eyes of my Shih Tsu forebears,
Though I've not got their silky long hair.
My curly white coat's cut in Bouchon Frise style.
I'm a show dog, as perhaps you're aware.

Yes, I am a Zuchon, and that is my calling.
It's no sinecure, I'd have you know.
For it is demanding and ever so tiring
To be perfect at show after show.

Postscript
Turn Me Around

Read my name in reverse.
There's the name of my Master.
I will do whatever He asks.
There are so many ways
I can be of His service.
I could be chosen for a number of tasks.

I might have to live rough
On the streets of a town,
To give warmth, and more, to give love.
My presence brings folk to
Engage with my owner.
P'rhaps the voice comes from above.

I may work as a guide
For the partially sighted.
I take them where they want to go.
I give purpose and joy
To a different owner,
Who may want to compete in some show.

I keep people healthy
By getting them out. I take
Them, once daily at least, for a walk.
I help the shy person
Come out of his shell; owners
Of dogs always learn how to talk!

If trained as a carer,
I can pick up the keys.
Sometimes, I'll answer the phone.
But much more than that,
I'm there, up for a chat,
For people who live on their own.

Mine might be a medical
Calling, to give warning
Of possible trouble ahead.
I raise people's spirits
By hospital visits.
Many people love patting my head!

See the light in my eyes.
I am here in disguise.
I am showing you Love,
This Love never dies.

Also by the Author

Pirouetting Hippos

'Hugely entertaining'.
'Quite unique'.
'As I read I chuckle often and marvel at your insights into life, persons, places and things'.

How Do I Look?

'So fresh and original'.
'I love your new book – so true to life and it makes me laugh'.
'You have exactly caught the current climate and mores in verse'.

You're Telling Me!

'Your poems not only bring a smile, they reach out to people with endearing warmth'.
'Full of perceptive capturing of life. To see humour in the commonplace, as you do, is delightful'.
'The poems contain much wisdom in a very entertaining packaging!'

Widening Horizons

'I admire your ability to express so aptly
what you have observed so keenly'.
'Your reflections lifted my spirits and
took me to a better place'.
'I really admire your ability to combine
lightness of touch and playfulness
with reflection'.

A Whiff of Rosemary

'I loved your poetry'.
'Congratulations on another wise
and witty volume'.
'You seize the incidents of life which we all
recognise and experience and reproduce them
to comic - and touching – effect. More please!'.

Stalking the Crilbit

'beautifully clever and crafted verse'.
'Loved your very intelligent and witty poems'.
'glorious poems'.